ON THE MOVE...

HOT AIR BALLOONS

By Tony Freeman

Consultant: Alan Blount, President
Balloon Federation of America

CHILDRENS PRESS, CHICAGO

Photo Credits:

Historical Pictures Service, Chicago, page 5
John Lancaster, pages 19, 20, 25, 27, 32, and 40
Tony Freeman, cover, pages 3, 7, 8 (2 photos), 9, 10, 11, 12 (2 photos), 13 (2 photos), 14, 16 (2 photos), 17, 18, 22, 24, 26, 28, 29, 30, 33, 34, 37, 38, 39, 41, 44

Library of Congress Cataloging in Publication Data

Freeman, Tony.
  Hot air balloons.

  (On the move)
  Includes index.
  Summary: Includes a brief history of hot air balloons
and describes how they work, the techniques of flying
them, and their uses.
    1. Hot air balloons—Juvenile literature. [1. Hot air balloons.
2. Balloons]   I. Title.   II. Series.
TL638.F74   1983   629.133'22   82-22087
ISBN 0-516-03891-5

What gets up very early in the morning and gives people a lift with its colorful spirit?

The answer is a hot air balloon.

It is also the answer to the question: "How do we have a lot of fun?"

People have wanted to fly like the birds since time began. It was in 1783 that two brothers in France noticed that smoke rose into the air from chimneys in their town. They thought the smoke had some special ability to rise into the air. They decided to fill a bag with smoke and see if it would rise from the ground.

It worked! So they built a large cloth bag and hung a metal pot beneath it. They built a fire in the pot so the smoke would fill the bag. It almost lifted them off the ground. On September 19, 1783 the two brothers, Joseph and Etienne Montgolfier, arranged for their first passengers to fly in a hot air balloon.

The passengers were a duck, a rooster, and a sheep. Only the rooster was afraid to fly in the balloon. But everyone already knew that he was a big chicken. The first chicken joke was born on that same day.

Their flight was a huge success. So a few
months later, on November 21, two men
made the first free flight in a balloon.
They flew about five miles across the
French countryside.

It was nearly 120 years later that the Wright brothers made their first controlled flight in an airplane. Two brothers made aviation history again.

Since the first balloon lifted away from the earth, we have learned a great deal about flying. The Montgolfier brothers were wrong to think that it was the smoke that caused the balloon to fly. It was really the hot air inside the cloth bag that made it rise into the sky.

You can check the fact that hot air rises. Measure the temperature of the air near the floor of a room with a thermometer. Check the temperature near the ceiling. You will find that the air at the top of the room is warmer. The air inside the balloon is much warmer than the air around the balloon, causing it to go up.

Modern hot air balloons use a large
burner fueled by propane gas to heat the
air in the bag. In modern balloons there is
no smoke at all and the balloon can
remain in the sky for one or two hours
with thirty gallons of fuel stored in ten
gallon tanks.

The flame of the burner shoots into a large opening at the bottom of the balloon. The bag, which is also called an envelope, is made of modern rip-stop nylon or polyester. It is a very strong fabric. It is also used for parachutes and hang gliders. You may own a sleeping bag or small tent made of rip-stop nylon or polyester.

Hot air balloons often fly very early in the morning. There are two reasons for this. The air is usually very still at this time of day. This makes it easier to fly balloons since they are easily blown around by the wind. And the morning air is usually cool. Remember, hot air rises. If the air around the balloon full of hot air is cool, the balloon rises more easily.

The cooler the air is, the more *lift* the balloon will produce. Lift means the ability of the balloon to carry weight from the ground into the sky. A balloon that can lift four people in the winter air might be able to lift only two people in the summer, when the air around the balloon is warmer. The air around the balloon is called *ambient air*.

The crew arrives at the launching site in the morning before sunrise. It takes two to four strong people to lift the balloon and basket from the truck to the ground. A few of the balloonists' trucks even have power tailgates to help unload and reload the balloon.

The crew has to unfold the huge balloon
on the ground. Then it is fastened to the
basket with stainless steel wires. The entire
balloon is set up on its side first. Then a
fan with a gasoline engine is started. It
blows cold air into the balloon to begin to
fill it up. The cold air does not rise so the
balloon stays on its side on the ground.

When it is filled, the pilot lights the large propane burner and points the flame into the envelope opening. As the air inside the bag starts to get warmer, the envelope rises.

Gradually, the basket tips up and the pilot and passengers get into it. Other crew members help hold the basket steady. They do not want the balloon to take off yet!

The pilot uses a checklist to make sure everything is working properly. He has to give a blast of flame from the burner from time to time to keep the balloon standing at attention. He cannot get it too warm, though, or it will take off before he wants it to.

In some balloons the pilot and his fellow fliers all must wear helmets for safety. Ballooning is a very safe sport, but landings can be bumpy at times. All sports call for safety steps to help us enjoy them.

"Hands off!"

The pilot shouts the command and the crew members let go of the basket. It lifts gently from the ground, slowly at first. If there is no wind, it goes almost straight up. A little breeze on the side of the big bag will make it travel with the wind as it rises.

Ballooning is a "free" sport in which people work with nature for their enjoyment and fun. Balloonists get the same thrill from teaming up with the wind and the sky that surfers do with waves, or sailors with the wind in their sails.

Since the pilot cannot see what is above him, he often gets help from his crew on the ground over a two-way radio. He can also see his shadow on the ground.

The pilot and crew ride in a basket made of wicker (reeds) or aluminum. Both are strong and light. Most of them can carry three or four people.

Balloonists like to fly together. Sometimes there will be forty or fifty balloons taking off within minutes of each other. The sky seems to be filled with colorful fabric Christmas-tree ornaments.

The view from one of the first balloons into the sky each day makes the others look like giant, colored mushrooms on the ground.

Balloons have the right-of-way. This means that other aircraft, such as airplanes, have to stay out of their way. This is because the balloon pilot can only control the up and down movement of his balloon with much sureness. Sideways movement is up to the direction of the winds in the sky.

The wind at one distance above the ground (*altitude*) may be blowing one direction. At a higher altitude, it may be blowing a different way. A pilot can check the wind with toy helium balloons before he launches the balloon.

Most balloons are about sixty feet tall
and nearly forty feet across. This is a big
object for the wind to blow against, so the
balloon has little choice but to travel at the
same speed as the wind.

There is really no top speed in a balloon. Because the wind and the balloon are traveling together, the people in the balloon do not feel the wind at all! It is possible to light a candle in the open basket of a balloon that is crossing over the ground at twenty-five miles per hour.

Things are different when the balloon lands, though. The basket has a solid bottom, but no wheels. If the wind is high when the balloon lands, the basket can bump across the ground at a high speed.

If this happens, the pilot can pull a long cord hooked to a panel or valve on the top of the balloon. The panel will open and release the hot air all at once. The balloon basket may land a little hard, but it will come to a stop instead of bouncing across the countryside.

Anybody can ride in a balloon. You can even learn to be a pilot of a balloon if you are age fourteen or older. Many people are pilots, but do not own balloons of their own. They are members of balloon clubs who share the cost of owning a balloon.

Other people will buy balloons and use
them as a business. They give people rides
and earn money to pay for the balloon
that way. Some of them will go up in their
balloon with signs on the side to advertise
a store or product. Many offer lessons so
that others can learn to fly.

A balloon costs about as much as a nice sports car or a speedboat. It costs about as much to fly a balloon (for fuel, mostly) as it does to drive an automobile.

It is very exciting to float quietly above houses, farms, and parks. Balloons usually fly at an altitude of about five hundred to one thousand feet. It is fun to see all the people on the ground looking up at the balloon and waving.

Each balloon must have a chase vehicle. This is usually the truck or van that carries the balloon to the launch site. It should have at least two people in it. One watches the balloon while the other drives and watches the road. The chase vehicle meets the balloon when it lands and brings it home.

While the balloon is in flight the pilot will have to use the burner to give blasts of flame now and then. How often he does it depends on the weight in the basket and the ambient temperature. The sound of the burner makes a loud whooshing noise. But it does not hurt the ears of those in the balloon's basket.

It takes about ten seconds for the balloon to begin to rise after the heat is added. The pilot must learn to judge this and not get the balloon too hot. The hottest it gets is usually about 250 degrees Fahrenheit inside the bag. That is probably the lowest setting on the oven in your house.

In calm winds a good pilot can land his balloon on an egg and not break it! One pilot landed on the end of a diving board of a swimming pool. A favorite trick of many pilots is to land on the surface of a lake and make the basket glide across the top of the water.

31

Once the balloon lands, the people in the basket cannot get out and walk away. If they did, the balloon would suddenly be lightened and take off into the sky again!

When balloons fly in the rain, they do not act as big umbrellas as you might think. The rain collects on the bag and runs off onto the crew getting them all wet. A good pilot does not fly when it might rain.

Balloons have been used for many things besides flying for fun. During a war in 1848, bombs were hooked to balloons and they were set free without pilots. The balloons headed for the enemy. Then the wind changed direction and the bombs floated back over the people who had built them. This was not tried again by those people.

Balloons were used in the American Civil War to help spot troop movements.

During World War II the Japanese tried hooking bombs to balloons. Several bombs even made it to the United States.

Balloons gave other people ideas, too. Some balloons were given motors. Other balloons were filled with gas, which was lighter than air. These did not have to be hot to rise into the sky. They worked like the balloon you might buy at the zoo or circus. These special balloons often had motors on them and they could be steered through the air. The word *dirigible* means steerable so they are called dirigibles. The Goodyear blimp is this kind of balloon. These balloons are stretched into a cigar shape, since, if you put a motor on a round balloon, it would only spin in a circle.

Balloonists are very friendly with each
other. They have contests and games called
rallies. At a rally one of the favorite games
is called "hare and hound." The first
balloon takes off and lands. He is the
"hare." The winner is the "hound" balloon
that can throw a marker closest to the
"hare."

Another kind of contest calls for the balloonist to drop bean bags or bags of flour onto a target. There are many other types of contests that test a pilot's skill at navigation.

Rallies and championships are held around the world and balloon teams from many countries may come together for the larger ones.

One of the biggest gatherings of balloons in the world is held in Albuquerque, New Mexico each October. About four hundred balloons will fly each day!

The U.S. National Championships are held in Indianola, Iowa in August of each year. Only the best one hundred pilots in the country may compete in the championships.

The color, the fresh air, the excitement of flying high above the rest of the world all add up. They add up to make ballooning one of the best things there is to do in all the world.

Terms used by hot air balloonists

Aeronaut: a balloonist

Ambient air: the air around the outside of the balloon

Altimeter: an instrument that tells how high the balloon is

Altitude: distance above the ground

Ascend: go up

Bag: the fabric bubble of the balloon

Basket: the wicker or aluminum box in which the passengers ride

Burner: the device that burns the fuel

Charts: maps

Chase vehicle: truck that follows and picks up the balloon

Compass: an instrument that shows direction of travel

Crown: the center of the top of a balloon

Descend: come down

Dirigible: a stretched-out steerable balloon

Envelope: see Bag

Fuel: propane gas similar to kitchen stove gas

Gasoline engine fan: used to start blowing up the balloon

Ground speed: how fast balloon is traveling over the land

Hand-held burner: used to begin heating the air in the balloon during setup, rarely used with modern systems

Helmet: protection for passengers' heads

Land: return to earth

Lift: the balloon's ability to rise with weight in the basket

Log book: a record of flights

Montgolfier brothers: men who built the first balloon

Mooring or tethering: tying balloon in place

Morning air: calm and cool air for better flights

Nylon: light, strong fabric to make balloon envelopes or bags

Pilot: the person who flies the balloon

Polyester: fabric similar to nylon

Pyrometer: a temperature gauge for the envelope

Propane: fuel

Radio: method pilot uses to talk to the ground crew

Rally: meeting of balloonists for races and games

Rate of climb indicator: an instrument that tells pilot how fast he is ascending or descending

Rigging: equipment and ropes, cables that hold the basket to the balloon

Safety line: a heavy cord that can open the flap or valve at the top of the balloon to release the heat

Sparker: used to light the burner

Stair step: stopping at various altitudes to check wind direction

Volume of balloon: about 70,000 cubic feet—about as much air as in enough footballs to fill 7 or 8 school classrooms.

Wind speed: the speed at which the wind travels over the ground (A balloon usually cannot launch in winds over 10 miles per hour.)

More information? Contact
The Balloon Federation of America
P.O. Box 346
Indianola, Iowa 50125

INDEX

About the Author

Tony Freeman has taught photography at Anaheim High School in Anaheim, California since 1962. He feels that a teacher should be active in the field he is teaching. For this reasons, as well as to help feed his wife and six children, he has provided several thousand photographs to publications across the nation as a free-lance photographer for the last fifteen years.

He began writing several years ago when several magazines asked for words with his photographs, and has since become a busy writer-photographer. Freeman has written over half a dozen books for Childrens Press.

Freeman has been active with his children in Boy and Girl Scouting, school bands, and church activities. He is around young people so much that he considers himself a child at heart. So it was only natural that he turn to writing and illustrating children's books. He gets great pleasure from learning new things and sharing these discoveries with young people, both in his classroom and in his books.